DINOSAUR DASH!

Written by Charlotte Raby
Illustrated by Douglas Holgate

Mr and Mrs Diplodocus felt sorry for their son, Plod.

Today was the dinosaur dash, but Plod was dreading it.

Plod was upset by an unpleasant gang led by T-Rex.
They bullied Plod and his friends, Steg and Rap.

All month they had made the other young dinosaurs feel rubbish about the contest.

"And what will it be like *after* they have won?" Plod wondered.

"Then we must work as a group and not let them win," said Steg.

"Yes!" agreed Rap.

If only it was that easy …

Who will win?

Stegosaurus
Steg

How heavy? .... 2722 kg
How tall? .... 4.3 m
How fast? .... Slow but steady

What he is like
- Cool spikes
- Will not give up

Diplodocus

Plod

How heavy? .... 22 680 kg
How tall? .... 9.1 m
How fast? .... Slow!

What he is like
- Very long neck
- Good swimmer

Oviraptor
Rap

How heavy? .... 36 kg
How tall? .... 0.9 m
How fast? .... Super fast

What he is like
- Quick
- Small
- Clever

Tyrannosaurus Rex
T-Rex

How heavy? .... 7258 kg
How tall? .... 7 m
How fast? .... Not as fast as he feels he is!

What he is like
- Feels he is perfect!
- Looks frightening

Albertosaurus
Bert

How heavy? .... 2722 kg
How tall? .... 4.5 m
How fast? ..... Quick and then very slow

What he is like
- Good at hiding in bushes

Allosaurus
Al

How heavy? .... 1814 kg
How tall? .... 5.2 m
How fast? .... Quick to begin and then slow

What he is like
- Very strong
- Never gives up!

The dinosaurs got ready to run.
They pushed and shoved as they lined up.

T-Rex was off. Al shoved ahead.
Rap sped after them.
Plod and Steg lumbered along behind, with Bert.

Sometime later they got to the lake. T-Rex and Al were huffing and puffing. But where was Bert?

Plod saw Rap somersault into the lake. He jumped in with Steg and swam.

Plod and his crew were just ahead as they got out of the lake.
But T-Rex had planned a mean trick.

Bert jumped out of the bushes and shoved them all over!
T-Rex ran ahead.
"Losers!" he scoffed.

Mr and Mrs Diplodocus peered down and saw what the bullies had done. So Plod and his friends won the contest!